The Persistence of History

Also by Graeme Hetherington
Remote Corners (Twelvetrees Publishing, 1986)
In the Shadow of Van Diemen's Land (Cornford Press, 1999)
Life Given (Ginninderra Press, 2002)
A Tasmanian Paradise Lost (Walleah Press, 2003)
A Post-Colonial Boy (Fullers Publishing Pty Ltd, 2017)
At Large (Ginninderra Press, 2017)
An Inherited Epic of Gilgamesh (Ginninderra Press, 2019)
Another Love, Another Life (Ginninderra Press, 2020)
The Divided Self (Ginninderra Press, 2022)

Graeme Hetherington

The Persistence of History

The Persistence of History
ISBN 978 1 76109 634 1
Copyright © text Graeme Hetherington 2023
Cover image: David Keeling

First published 2023 by
GINNINDERRA PRESS
PO Box 3461 Port Adelaide 5015
www.ginninderrapress.com.au

Contents

Preface	7

1

The Poem I Was Born to Write	11
Postcard: for RM	14
After *Veil 1991–92* (1)	16
After *Veil 1991–92* (2)	18
After *Gate 1994* (1)	20
After *Gate 1994* (2)	21

2

After *Curios 1999* and *Everything Must Go 2003*	25
After *Domestic View 1991*	27
Song of a Sublimated Psychopath	28
For Queen Elizabeth II	30

3

After *Hazards Forest 2006–07* and *White Tree 2006–07*	33
After *Industry 1991*	35
After *Through the Trees 2001*	36
After *Two Day Trip – Call Home 2003* (1)	38
After *Two Day Trip – Call Home 2003* (2)	39
After *Landcare Trees, Jericho, Tasmania 2000*	40

4

After *Young Couple In Developing Landscape 1988*	43
After *Frontier Foundation 1994*	45
After *To the Island 1989*	46
A Tasmanian-English Tale	47
After *Der Zustand (the state of things) 1993*	48
After *Friendly Beaches Forest 2007*	50

5

Letter	53
Blossom (2)	55
After *Late Afternoon Walk 2007*	56
After *Nostalgia 1998*: for H	57
Czech Family Life: for Ivana	59

6

After Paintings Featuring White Tablecloths	63
After *Shroud 1994*	64
After *The Cunning Fox 1998*	65
After *Early Morning 2003*	67
After *Other Edens 1998*	69
After *Plenty 1994*	70
A Second Response to *Other Edens 1998* and *Plenty 1994*	72

7

Twists and Turns of the Worm	77
After a Lloyd Rees Image	80
Sixty Lines For Sixty Years	81
Nightmare in Brown	84
Atlas Drive: What's In a Name?	86

8

After *A Bigger Bonsai 2000*	89
After *Empty Gesture 1988*	92
After *Gate 1994* (3)	93
After *The Persistence of History* 1994	95
After *Study For Road In 2002*	99
After *End of the Road 2002*	100

Preface

Many thanks are due to David Keeling since many of the poems in this collection were written in response to his paintings as reproduced in David Hansen's book *David Keeling* published by Quintus Publishing in 2007.

It should also be noted that these poems represent, quite simply, my personal response to some of his work, as one Tasmanian to another, so to speak, and are not to be seen in any way as a critical appreciation of his art.

Thanks are also due to Ralph Spaulding for his valuable suggestions, to Elizabeth Love for her typing and to Ginninderra Press for previous publication of some of the poems.

1

The Poem I Was Born to Write

British Empire legacy

1

Van Diemen's Land convict kin thrown
Out of Paradise, their home in
England, as was Lucifer by

God from heaven, I wonder if,
Spiritually bruised, I view
My left thumbnail splitting apart

As vestige of a cloven hoof
To equate with my inner state,
Choose pyjamas of mixed hues that

Evoke beaten flesh to go with
My Hell's Gates prison origins,
And if a purely bright red pair

Induces dreams of bursting in
To flames from which I wake intact
Because I am inured to them?

2

Disdaining nose, cruel thin mouth in
Portraits suggest the governor of
Van Diemen's Land, George Arthur, whom

I strip of other titles, was
An autocrat contemptuous of
The sweepings from England he ruled

With hangings floggings ball and chain,
Thrilling to pain knifing his arse
As with puritanical zeal

He gloried in his duty done,
Whose buttocks as he held himself
Stiffly aloof were tightly clenched,

As though to defecate demeaned,
Was something only lowly folk
Like my convict kin dumped there did,

Whom, distastefully, as the turds
Of curs toed aside, he'd dismiss,
His boot's imprint much deeper on

The island's foully conceived soul.
Thus on the throne I fantasise,
Fear the door being broken down

By secret police come to drag
Me off to be grilled then shot for
Thoughts harmful to a state evolved

From his harsh ways and able to
Sniff out descendants of old lags.
And always mixed in with these thoughts,

My business half-done, trousers down
Around my ankles as I strain,
There's toilet training, gloomy strict

Indoctrinated mother who
With hers religion has deranged,
Hiss either side, right in my ears,

Smacking pinching as I strive to
Expel the enemy within,
The Devil as a vile brown snake,

Fit *leitmotiv* for a Hell's Gates'
Port Arthur-bequeathed coat of arms.
Small wonder then my need to fight

Off feeling I've turned into shit.
And does my Mother Country lost,
Crazy though it may seem, explain

To some extent at least my sense
Of shifting into female shape
To rectify and compensate?

Postcard: for RM

Your postcard of two whale's teeth set
Against a pitch-black background could
Be greetings from Van Diemen's Land,

Forming, as they do for me, bred
From folk transported there, into
The Devil's horns, that next become

The temptingly innocent white
Columns of an entrance to his
Den of iniquity, bright as

A toothpaste-ad smile welcoming
One to pass through Hell's Gates, each post
Scrimshawed with a dancing pair in

Victorian dress, and too close for
Comfort about to fall into
The abyss, coupling as they go.

I see it framed above the bed
Of my wowser grandmother as
A stern moral admonishment

In company with the many more
Than Ten Commandments hanging there,
A woman so against joy she

Became the butt of family jokes
At her henpecked husband's expense,
A man twice her size chipped away

To early death by strictures that
Denied him humour, gambling, drink,
Though tippling on the quiet herself,

One claiming she burnt Moby Dick
Because the novel's name fouled her
Collection of Wesleyan tracts.

After *Veil 1991–92* (1)

A veil of subterfuge, deceit,
Imbrued with colours brighter than
Those in the ores blasted from rock,

That usually hides earth's ruined face,
Hangs swept aside, in folds that say
'Let's try "honesty is the best

Policy" for a change, to see
If it pays higher dividends.'
But humankind can't tolerate

Reality for long, and so,
Fluttering, it waits, ready to be
Whipped permanently back across,

Again to mask the treeless hills,
The sulphurous wasteland and bones
Of blacks massacred for access

To wealth that will feed vanity
And conceit valued above all,
Of men lost to silicosis,

Alcoholism, because of
Nothing-else-to-do-save-drink, stark,
Deprived social environments,

To accidents the shaming lack
Of basic safety measures, greed
And sheer indifference explain, till

The seepage of truth soaks and turns
It into a lack-lustre shroud
Reflective of a worked-out mine.

After *Veil 1991–92* (2)

Timber mill owner burnt out in
New Zealand, then Tasmania's south
And north, Grandad under a cloud,

Growing darker with each 'mishap',
Moved at sixty-five with a weak
Heart to work hidden, buried in

The isle's West Coast underground mines,
Though already well-camouflaged
By his doubtful, suspicious past

For where bad weather, crimes denied
Were part of life. A comedown for
Four daughters closeted among

The drunken human debris of
A town with outlandish vile Van
Diemen's Land Hell's Gates' origins,

Who all later became disturbed,
Medically, confinably mad,
His wowser-wife, my granny wore

Black hat with veil raised only to
Terrify me, 'a wicked child',
With chalky white crumbled face like

A quarry's ore, which. blasted out
Rained on our rusted phlegm-green roof.
Otherwise she kept it down, shamed,

In mourning for fetching up there,
As my mother used curtains, blinds
To stop Old Nick from looking in.

Therefore, in need of healing, I
See your drape's colours, brilliant as
Joseph's coat, the Covenant's rich

Rainbow hues, as Art's power to
Redeem, even the foreground's bones
Of my kin faintly lit by it,

While the pyromaniac's are
Transfigured beyond all, since his
Love alone warmed me as a child.

After *Gate 1994* (1)

No pearly gate of Paradise,
This entrance is to Satan's realm,
And made of faintly visible,

Thin, overly ornate wrought iron
Patterned and scrolled with foetal shapes
That have no future, it's the fore-

Ground to a landscape of dry mounds
Arranged in pairs like shorn-off breasts,
And satirises all our weak

Efforts to keep at bay and save
Ourselves from Mother Earth's profound
And irreversible defeat,

From her massive mastectomy
And bounty rendered null and void.
While in the heavens storm clouds bring

My West Coast of Tasmania Hell's
Gates' narrow kill-joy Methodist
Grandmother scarily to mind,

Her idea of foul weather as
Jehovah's thunderous face of wrath,
The day of reckoning at hand.

After *Gate 1994* (2)

Gates more unlike each other I
Can't easily imagine! Mine
In childhood was a stock-in-trade,
Solidly old-fashioned one, made

To span entrances to drives, yards,
Let, keep, in or out. And it served,
As simple wire and metal, plain,
No-nonsense structure as stage for

Unambiguous enactments
Of dramas of the heart, since there,
Clambering up despite parents' 'No!'
For fear of damage to it, I

Would wait for Grandad's hug on his
Way home from work. But your wrought iron,
Fussily elaborate affair,
Refined beyond belief is frail,

No obstacle to anything,
An artistically precious piece,
Suggesting people behind it
Of nightmarish complexity,

Indecisive and paralysed,
Spaghetti-minded as they gaze
Bewildered and confused through it
At devastated nature in

The form of heaps of mullock on
Their doorstep, ornamental steel
Leaves clinging to the wispy frame
All that remains of foliage.

Which gives to our two barriers
At least a view of ravaged earth
In common, rocks rained on our roof
From blasting in a quarry not

Much more than a stone's throw away,
As was a lake of grey quicksand
From the mine in which drunkards drowned,
Though I had worse pollutants in

Bully boys living opposite
I looked out for in terror as
I unchained my protective friend
And left on the long walk to school.

2

After *Curios 1999* and *Everything Must Go 2003*

If it had been my lot to live,
As my unhappy mother did,
Beneath a mountain blocking out
Escape into a view of sea

Or sky, upon a foothill cleared
And levelled dead-flat to create
A government housing estate,
I would have done the same, gone mad,

Drawn blinds and curtains, opted for
'The Great Indoors' among a mix
Of in-all-shades of cardboard-brown,
Affordably cheap thinnish sticks

Of furniture. For company I
Too might in bitterness have bought
Shiny black bulbous skull shapes, bowls
Of venom standing on about-

To-scurry spider legs, and on
Poised, elegantly supple, curved
Octopus tentacles. They brought
Back memories of the head, she said,

Of spastic cousin Ian shaved
For surgery, and Uncle Neil's
Dark from a booze-induced burst vein.
And I too, lonely and withdrawn,

Grown just as desperate and inclined
To perversity, would have named
And talked to them for years on end,
But I had better luck, a kind

Of clearance of the mind, and threw
Life in the suburbs on the tip,
Both her insane interior
And world beyond the lounge peeped at:

Garage and jumble sales, those draw-
Card weekend technicolour shows
Of gimcrack bits and pieces, junk
No sooner acquired than piled up

On corpse-grey concrete pavements for
Ten dollars, dear at half the price,
And which she always saw as too
Beneath her ever to attend,

And finally just couldn't for
The angst that shook her at the thought,
A panic attack killing as
She clung at ninety to an arm-

Less curio for comfort in
Her hour of need, the favourite of
The collection, which though poisonous
She still preferred to other folk.

After *Domestic View 1991*

Dark blue funereal drapes drawn
Aside hang crookedly in folds
Still fluttering, as though someone

In gloomy undertaker mood,
Misanthropic to their cold core,
Anxiously wanting to look out

The window unseen, has just now
Stepped back, the scene luckily free
Of humans stored in their mind's eye:

The sky a sickly poisonous black
Mixed in with yellow to portend
This as the final day of life,

While onto a urine-green land-
Scape with a stream so silted up
With brown that it resembles shit,

They project a government-planned
Housing development, homes filled,
Not with white goods, but mounds of dust

From a mountain ground down for them,
Mother Earth the ultimate corpse
With nothing to be buried in.

Song of a Sublimated Psychopath

After the television series *Killing Eve*

1

Though bravely hands on, slaughtering with
The sword, and not like me with pen,
I'm smitten by Villanelle, cool-

As-a-cucumber psychopath
Hired by amoral governments
As an assassin, who shoots Eve,

Archetypal mother, because
She scorned her love, as I in poems
For the same crime in childhood still

Bump mine off. Both under threat, she
Physically and I mentally,
We share an aesthetic that helps

Us in the battle to survive:
The streamlined killer instinct of
The guiltless compassion-free shark

That guarantees the job gets done,
The contract flawlessly fulfilled,
And in my case maximum power

Harnessed for exorcism in
Straight-down-the-line, honed-to-the-bone,
Efficient, therapeutic verse.

2

I love Villanelle because she
Did a poo, at the age of three,
In her mother's shoe, a big one,

Before she was given away,
Only to return and kill her,
Burn, family inside, the house down,

Then flee for the lick of her life.
Dobbed in by my brother, whom I
Had gone for with a knife, not to

Mention murderous impulses for
The others of my kin, I failed,
Just managing to set the fire,

And instead, while safely abroad
Sublimated this in poems.
But even so it was enough

For me to see myself in her,
Comforted to feel less alone
As a complete and utter turd.

For Queen Elizabeth II

With nothing beautiful in our
Cheerless home to engage my love
Except the warmly colourful

Women's Weekly covers, you won
As fairy-tale Princess, and then
As smiling Queen my childhood heart

That my birth-mother's coldness left
Empty for abstract joy to fill.
And now, the goose-pimpling beat of

Muffled drums timing the slow march
Of those attending your death, thrills
Me through and through, who nothing felt

At hers who gave me life, the ranks
Swaying in perfect unison
As trees do in a gentle breeze,

As you, Elizabeth, still my
Outlet for all that's best in me
Are farewelled worldwide on TV.

3

After *Hazards Forest 2006–07* and *White Tree 2006–07*

It's not the spindly stands of trees
As such that bring on my unease.
I'm from the same poor sandy soil
And understand their hairy twig-
Sharp, twisted anorexic look,

The sinisterly thickening mist
That as it drenches them enshrouds.
In schooldays I read on a wind-
Blown page of *Truth* impaled by one
About George Haigh, the acid bath,

Blood-drinking English murderer
I thought I'd grow up to become
And didn't bat an eyelid or
So much as tell a living soul.
But since I've lost my West Coast of

Tasmania's Hell's Gates' childhood cool,
My devilish attitudes, his face,
I also took in with the words,
Might just resurface and now scare,
Even unhinge me in these woods,

And your she-oak with loose white bark,
As poisonously puffy as
My idea of a leper could
Turn powdery at a touch and swarm
With vile black Edgar Allan Poe-

Imagined things right up into
My facial orifices, till,
Pouring through, my brain, teeming with
Horror enough already bursts
Among the skewering foliage.

After *Industry 1991*

Mine manager and handyman,
My father's aptitude for all
Things practical, and his belief

That Nature was God-given to
The human species to exploit,
To cut and dig, confront me in

Your painting where machinery parts,
Brutally superimposed, wheel
Over doomed Lake Pedder as though

They constitute the universe.
Set stiffly like sheet metal in
A plain, the dammed still waters glare

Malevolently with revenge,
And damn, if you'll forgive the pun,
The imprisoning, man-shaped hills,

The once green-wooded slopes that now,
Drought-brown and cowering confirm
My identity, that I'm blessed,

Not cursed to be without those skills
That first harness and then destroy,
Of which my old man was so proud.

After *Through the Trees 2001*

Your painting of an emerald space
Set in the woods evokes the time
I caddied for my father till
He sacked me at the thirteenth as
A scapegoat for his rotten play,

Outraged that I, his ten-year-old
'Useless arrangement of a son'
The kids at school confirmed with 'ciss',
Had seen it all the way to there.
Also, and more specifically,

I lost the job for failing to
Retrieve the small white costly pills
Skewed into creeks and long grass on
The Rosebery course; for handing him,
Out of sheer nervousness to please,

The 'masher' instead of an iron;
For not replacing his divots,
So many clumps of turf clubbed out
That partners jokingly invoked
Rabbits and wombats, else he'd dug,

Turned sods to start a veggie patch;
And, crime of crimes, for dumping to
Chase butterflies or have a spell,
His bag made heavier with beer
In case the nineteenth had run out.

And to this day I hope that in
The next world he forever drives,
Like Sisyphus and Tantalus,
Straight down the middle of a tree-
Lined hazardous fairway onto

The eighteenth, the last lovely green,
Praying to God to hole-in-one,
Redeem disaster and save face,
And always finds, as in your work,
There's nowhere to bury the ball.

After *Two Day Trip – Call Home 2003* (1)

The unspoilt natural-looking pull-
In place of shading trees and sand
Spread thinly, smoothly like a beach

Has made the one car parked there seem
A useless heap of metal stored
For no good reason in that shape

Now it's motionless, function lost.
Or does it, with the windows veiled
By sunlight serve to hide someone?

The driver with back turned to it,
And suspiciously out of hearing, is
Our tantalising clue as he,

Like his stationary wheels, strikes
An ugly, discordant note in
This setting, slouching overweight

And shabbily attired to phone
His home, perhaps to catch the wife
Also cheating while he's away,

The tension arising from our
Fruitless speculation resolved
By wanting him, his vehicle,

With dolly bird concealed or not,
To leave a scene that will refresh
Once its emptiness is complete.

After *Two Day Trip – Call Home 2003* (2)

I see my father, brought up to
Date with a mobile in your work
Of a typical travelling sales-

Man, slouching out of earshot of
His car, as sleepily, flat from
The beer he took on board at lunch

Treating a well-heeled client who
Didn't live up to the outlay,
He keys in, calling the wife, my

Mother to say work has delayed,
A passenger in the form of
A dolly bird from Myer's scent

Counter, shiny and tinny as
The small cheap vehicle his firm
Provides, out of sight in the back.

After *Landcare Trees, Jericho, Tasmania 2000*

Too rotten now to take a nail,
Let alone bear the weight of Christ,
A pair of trees with no hope of

Spring's leaves reprieving from decline
Inevitably into dust,
Yet standing close to upright still

In memory of once-towering height,
Will in their own good time curl up
Their roots as humans do their toes.

Meanwhile they have each other to
Enjoy, the scene suggesting they've
Banished another to the far

Distance for being more decayed
And stinking of the grave than them.
Or has two's company three's a crowd

Resulted in its fate to lean,
From the top, like a head, against
The empty unsustaining sky,

Exhausted from sheer loneliness,
Wavering, hesitating to take
A first step in its dance with death?

4

After *Young Couple In Developing Landscape 1988*

Your portrait of a youthful pair
Posed toffee-nosed, smug among signs
Of rurally provincial art
And crudely cruel history that's warped
The Tasmanian descendants of

The felons of Van Diemen's Land
Could easily be seen as one
Of Graeme and Susan Hetherington
Blown in as Lord and Lady Muck
To scornfully ignore such things

As just colonial bad taste.
The first a native white escaped
To culturally richer Greece
In an attempt to change his roots,
The second measuring all by her

Superior pom origins,
They're blind to Glover-eucalypts
Snaking out to asphyxiate
Them for their studied arrogance,
To bones of blacks lying around,

Waiting to resurrect and trip
Them into a convict-dug pit
That in conceit they overlook
Although close to the edge of it,
Emblem of their crowd-pleasing fall

Into the hell of splitting up,
Bankruptcy, children lost, when she,
Disoriented, dispossessed,
Twice broke down crying out for home,
And he, already there, if but

Contemptuously, cooly took
The opportunity to get
Rid of them, being able to
Wrestle the mess into a poem,
Lives irreversibly destroyed.

After *Frontier Foundation 1994*

Again the woman in one of
Your paintings could be my first wife,
The archetypal whingeing Pom

Of doubtful pioneering stock
As gormlessly caved-in she sits
Slumped and supported by an arm

On a building's foundation bricks
In the nearly empty countryside
Of Van Diemen's Land, the Devil's isle,

Her new home. Quite unable to
Make a go of it, depression has
Deepened from life among the bones

Of murdered blacks beneath her feet,
And strengthening her attitude
Of 'nothing's left to make me try'

Brought on psychotic episodes,
Hallucinations to judge from
Her startled look, the other hand

Raised in terror from the surprise:
Five thin dark lines encroaching on
The foreground like prongs of a pitch-

Fork she alone sees the rest of,
And who wields it, moving towards.
Her from beyond the picture's frame.

After *To the Island 1989*

Black-framed, the scene's a mourning card,
Since I could be the man who rows
The woman to a rock shaped as

Tasmania upside down. My wife,
I wed too quickly to know her
Untransplantable English side,

She stands to rock the boat and take
Advantage of ambivalence,
My deep-rooted conflict about

Whether this outcrop of forlorn
Alcatraz-like rock in the south,
My native isle, is truly home,

Her mind made up she'll drown before
Setting foot there, yet staying till
After seven years broken by

Clinics, ECT, me, I took
Her and our girls back, leaving them
In London where we'd met, for what

Then seemed would be our mutual good,
Only to learn, as it turned out,
I'd circumscribed my life with grief.

A Tasmanian-English Tale

Emotionally volatile, split
In my allegiance, I dumped 'rule-
Britannia' wife and daughters back

In 'the old Dart', avenging kin
Transported to Van Diemen's Land
By turning its vile origins

That blighted my home on their head.
Then you, another of her ilk,
Mother Country born and bred, yet

Not imperious, and by luck
Also deserted, left to care
For two young children, came in from

The garden sensuously wet,
Time standing still as my held breath.
Sublime in all your Englishness,

Transfigured beyond history's reach,
Red roses in your hands not gouts
Of felons' blood but glistening jewels,

It seemed to make good loss, restore
My convict-and-the-lady dream
Where all's forgiven and 'the stain'

Of criminality's erased,
Now that I'd evened up the score
And my proud heart had grown contrite.

After *Der Zustand (the state of things)* 1993

How harrowing to view a hare
Hung by hind paws in front of bleak
Hills more certainly dead than it,

The eye in profile open, ears
Alert and front legs ready to
Bound off if cut down. As further proof,

There's not one blowfly buzzing near
With foul intent. But where to live
In such a world denuded of

All save the rubbish of the past,
History's detritus and a strand
Of fence wire underneath which hangs

'*Der Zustand*' or 'the state of things',
Evoking concentration camps
Like Auschwitz-Birkenau with its

Entrance gate's infamously scrolled,
Equally matter of fact, bland
Ironic words of welcome? Or

Perhaps the whole polluted earth's
A gaol, and we, the inmates, need
In our degeneracy to

Have images of animals
Suggesting that the purely white,
Perky erect tail would be docked,

The similarly coloured gut,
Abundant with its young, slit wide
Before releasing it to flee?

After *Friendly Beaches Forest 2007*

I felt at risk on entering this
Ironically named painting, since
Thin bare, black crooked saplings seemed
About to straighten and become

Snakes standing on their tip of tail.
Outraged and swaying, darting heads
This way and that to strike at me,
They were the same six-footer I'd

So wounded with stones as a boy
That rearing it showed tiger stripes,
Hissed, barked I fancied as a child
With whooping cough before it fell

Into a dusty crumpled heap.
Gingerly disentangling with
A long stick, I slung it beside
Others over a strand of fence

Wire to be added to the score
Of killed in that summer's contest,
To twitch and keep the flies off till
It died at sunset as believed.

5

Letter

Dear 'Murky' Murgatroyd Jim Crow,
A throwback to Van Diemen's Land
Grotesquerie, your Hitler mo,
That's only half the hair around

The woman's part you wish you had,
Assures you of a knife between
The ribs on Hobart's waterfront
One of these anti-fascist nights.

Why you don't grow a tuft beneath
The lower lip, complete your need,
I'll never know. A closet poof,
You worked the dark State Library stacks

For arse until thrown out on yours,
And now you shuffle, crippled, down
The Bay Road looking for a toss.
Or are you Jack the Ripper, his

Reincarnation fetched up on
The Fatal Shore in search of tarts
To cut up in Whitechapel style,
Then, as a variation sign

Them 'mother whom I never loved'?
I also see you perched low down
Upon a tree, waiting for me
To come to grief and fall face up,

A Vandemonian sheephead,
From which you'd pick the eyes to get
Into my brain. This letter's in
Similarly sinister vein

To others written since you sent,
As editor, my poems back
On moral grounds, to again ask
What's your entitlement to preach?

Blossom (2)

for E

Suspended in a saucer filled
With water, a camellia's head
As present for my birthday failed

To give me joy, since my response,
After politely thanking you,
Was to recall how I'd lost mine,

My cool, contesting rather than
Showing indifference as boys teased,
Feminising me with the nick-

Name 'Blossom'. And when you'd left, crest-
Fallen that I still hadn't come
To terms with the past, raving on

About how Orpheus's sang
Torn off and floating down a stream,
I threw your gift into a bin,

Casting you, though kindness itself,
As Salome and Judith to
My St John the Baptist and King

Holofernes, as without thought,
Innocently you clenched and squeezed,
Secateuring through tough thick stem.

After *Late Afternoon Walk 2007*

So taken was I by the light,
The lyricism of the scene's
Blue clarity of summer sky,

Its sunny green expanse of lawn
And golden smooth-limbed she-oak grove
That seemed aspiringly to stretch

And strain upwards away from earth,
I failed at first to spot within
The undergrowth the two bald heads,

Dark glasses wrapped around despite
Shadows almost engulfing them.
And once the visual rot began

A yellow bike came quickly in
To view, festering against a tree,
Its back tyre like a snake curled mouth

To tip of tail contagiously
Thought of as black as buggery.
And round the copse hiding the pair

The grass became as rusty as
Needles used too often for drugs
Instead of gloriously lit,

Such blindness caused by need to see
The pure before the human burst
Upon the naive eye and fouled.

After *Nostalgia 1998*: For H

A trendy art curator from
The mainland sent to modernise
Hobart Museum's collection, you,

Despite my native loyalties, joked
That local talent, since not fit
To be hung should instead be drawn

And quartered. At the time we were
Viewing a born-and-bred's work that
You held was crude, when I perceived

The man in this painting as you,
A Noah sending forth the bird,
Assuming it would fly through glass,

And if it did, hoping in vain
It wouldn't melt down into ash,
As here his Ark's a large showcase,

Afloat not on floodwaters, but
Raised up on legs above a world
Baked brown and arid by the sun.

A witty image that conveys
In days of climate change a deep
Nostalgia for a way of life

Doomed to disappear, along with
You fried alive, I thought as on
I gazed, quite blown away by it,

When sensing my hostility
To your judgemental sneer, and out
Of pique that I dared disagree

With 'professional expertise'
You savagely ran knuckles down
My spine and brought me to my knees,

An otherwise unexplained act
You've got away with until this
Poem I've had up my sleeve for years.

Czech Family Life

For Ivana

The gladioli tightly sheathed,
Exemplifying the ideal
Of classical restraint when first

You placed them in our living room's
Scabbard-like vase, suddenly burst,
The whole bunch of them, five or six,

Into frozen jets of blood-red.
Swords drawn unwiped from an old feud,
As in the Aeschylean plays,

You could be Clytemnestra who
Slew husband Agamemnon for
Daughter Iphigenia's death,

I your lover Aegisthus, both
Killed by your son Orestes to
Avenge his father, and in turn

Is threatened by Electra, his
Sister now arguing with him
As he sits scowling at me for

Taking his divorced father's place,
So close to the vendetta in
His timeless masterpiece do our

Vexed family circumstances seem
To me, a classicist steeped in
Such gory texts for thirty years.

6

After Paintings Featuring White Tablecloths

Did you, I wonder, as a child
Feel all at sea one New Year's Day
As with a folded cloth you ran

To claim a table overhung
By trees near the beach? Was pride in
The chore spoilt knowing it would block

Others from eating there? If so,
Your works where only images
Of linen like a fall of snow

Lighten the mood, suggest yours too
Would brighten as you shook it out
And saw, not your clan's flag unfurled

And spread to selfishly exclude,
Or mother's carefully ironed starched best
As no more than a shroud to wrap

Happiness in, but sun-splashed sail
That billowing white launched your deep-
Down resolution thus to paint.

After *Shroud 1994*

Absence is presence felt, as with
The oinment-smooth, empty white shroud
Rinsed blue suspended in the sky
Above bare brown exhausted hills,
Unless its pinned folds slumping like

A hammock might wrap Jesus Christ.
His patience with our folly tried
Past breaking point, He cannot rise,
Bring back to life earth as in Blake's
'Jerusalem', where His pierced feet

Treading among, I love to think,
'The dark satanic mills' restored
The Mother Country's wastelands to
The pasturage of ancient times,
Fit for the Holy Lamb of God.

After *The Cunning Fox 1998*

I am the cunning fox that's leapt,
Lean and hungry, up from a smooth
Brown shit-soft looking floor onto

A freshly laundered plush white cloth
Covering a box shape that suggests
A coffin, tomb, an altar whose

Candles and Cross I as the Arch-
Fiend's familiar have knocked into
The unrelieved pitch darkness of

Background the scene is set against.
No smudging telltale paw-prints to
Testify to my presence, I

Sniff for food hoping to detect
Christ's body to devour, commit
The ultimate desecration,

Jeopardise the Resurrection,
Destroy the ritual of the Mass
By taking it so literally

Before slinking into the night,
Back to Van Diemen's Land, Hell's Gates'
Beginnings where convict forebears

Explain why I am prey to this
Criminal fantasy Old Nick
Would own, that overrides the thought

That here we have no such vile act,
But a stuffed Reynard mounted for
Display in Hobart Town's Museum.

After *Early Morning 2003*

Draped with a shadow-smudged white cloth,
The table startles set alone,
Just by virtue of being there,

In a small clearing won from trees
With sickly yellow feathery leaves
That easily could become the wings

Of Harpies that will further foul
The faintly shade-spoilt surface as
When Jason and the Argonauts

On a civilising quest paused
To shed armour and take their ease,
To dine in peace, were shat upon,

Their mission's purity debased.
Or will Yeats's 'rough beast' rise from
The undergrowth into this last

Outpost of hope, a moment of
Light in the painter's mind before
The shit factor kicked in and he

Realistically darkened it
With the merest hint of nightfall,
Bowing to our imperfect state,

Old Nick threatening to wipe his arse
On linen that first rivalled snow,
Or Gabbett from my Hell's Gates' past,

Making a pig of himself, stains,
With human flesh for his repast,
A shroud once worthy to wrap Christ?

After *Other Edens 1998*

The moment just before a storm,
Unnaturally calm, the sea
Waits tensely for the brooding sky

To split open, when God, enraged,
In the guise of a lightning flash
Will touch down on the water's face,

Zigzag over to what was once
Paradise set upon a shore,
Or else three partly submerged rocks

Mean His advent will take the form
Of rising triple-headed as
A monster to arrive where bread,

Bottle of wine, three glasses still
Upon a table prove He'd dined
With Adam and Eve prior to

Their Fall and Abel's murder, bones
Shown bleached on gangrenous-green ground.
And humankind now grown from bad

To worse, changed into wind He'll lift
The off-white cloth's skewed hem, tug, send
Flying to break beyond repair

The symbols of the sacrament,
His pledge eternally to love,
Care and forgive no matter what.

After *Plenty 1994*

Apocalyptic-looking clouds
Are echoed by the dirty brown
Hyena-slumping mullock mounds.

An image of a worked-out world,
Land-locked and claustrophobic, it
Begs for a cleansing sea and mocks

The Psalmist's 'mine eyes lift up to
The hills from whence cometh my help'.
And paradoxically set here,

A table sumptuously draped
In yellow, almost golden cloth
Only billionaires could provide,

The greedy ruling class that's failed
To lead responsibly and save
Hopeless humankind from itself,

With food spread carelessly, left to
Further the waste, evokes not Christ's
Last Supper, but rather their own,

The kings and presidents who've fled
Sudden catastrophe. And since
The ground's stained red, strewn with bones, it

Conceivably could also be
An altar's offering of just dregs,
Adding insult to injury

And thus unable to placate
History's oppressed and murdered folk
Whose spirits' cries for vengeance at

Long last have brought God down to Earth,
Where Judgement done He dines alone,
Seated invisibly apart

From what might be a drought-impaired
Lean Harvest Festival as well,
Arranged too late to please, if one

Small shining fragile half-filled glass
Placed isolated at the far
White lace-embroidered empty end

Can be asked to suggest Him there
To bear the weighty burden of
The painting's multilevel tale.

A Second Response to *Other Edens 1998* and *Plenty 1994*

Your tables aren't the 'groaning boards'
One might expect to go with our
Greedy materialistic times,

But with modest amounts of food
Arranged on clean fresh cloths await
The guests who'll stand to eat and talk,

Move freely around, absence of
Confining chairs capturing your
Mood of exhilaration, as,

Liberated from other chores,
Back and forwards you ran to fetch
And carry, making ready for

The gathering of your clan and friends
For an alfresco, picnic meal.
I see you pausing to admire

Your aesthetically pleasing work
Before people's enjoyment wrecked
With scattering, spillage, breakages,

Which brings me to the barren land,
The thunderous skies, deceptive sea,
Contexts for these otherwise calm

Expectant scenes that save them from
Unreality, as though you,
Like most boys, learnt that such events

Aren't pure unshadowed fun, and in
The ordinary course of things,
Like losing the sack, egg and spoon

Or three-legged race, are foretastes
Of 'trials and tribulations', what
Each life is called on to endure.

7

Twists and Turns of the Worm

(In the shadow of Van Diemen's Land)

An outgrowth of Van Diemen's Land,
Its ambience of guilt and shame
And deep inferiority,

Demons inherent in its name,
And hanging from the arsehole of
Australia despite Bass Strait's flush,

Where native products like myself
Exposed to insularity's
Soul-warping endless gossip are

Hypocrisy's worms always on
The turn in order to survive,
Tasmania was perfect for my

Mentor friend crush and confidant
James McAuley, feeling poorly
From bowel cancer and the grog,

To further his Cold War intrigues,
The island giving him stark grief-
Tormented, enigmatic poems,

An ever-darkening sinister,
As well as pious verse that sang
The praises of the Catholic Church

As sanction for his ruthlessness
On behalf of threatened ideals,
That involved splitting Labor in

The paranoid battle against
The legions of the Anti-Christ.
Hal Porter in *The Tilted Cross*

And I in this have got it right:
A convict-, Devil-poisoned speck
Upon the water's face attracts

The disturbed, becoming home for
Angst-ridden lady-poets who
Worsen their lives with fantasies

Of being shagged and torn to bits
By lions in a suburban cage;
For pommy painter Glover whose

Club feet and thuggish look belonged,
As did his serpentining gum
Tree boughs, providing camouflage

For Lucifer and capturing
The twist endemic to the isle,
Of Lady Jane's mind, so obsessed

With killing snakes that when she hen-
Pecked to emasculate her spouse,
The Governor she wished to be,

She added 'Thomas' to 'Sir John'.
These limbs also evoke the 'S'
In Smythe, the question mark about

The smarmy, simpering, sniggering bard
Called Adrian or Adrienne,
Since man or woman none can tell,

So clever are the games he plays,
A net-worker who'd cut the throat
Of granny to get into print,

Discarding local friends to dine
With fly-by-night celebrities
If it meant forwarding his poems,

Who, editing with this one aim
Definitively bears out that
Tassie's still crippled by its past.

After a Lloyd Rees Image

Thanks for the fairy-tale postcard,
But I'm afraid it didn't blow
Me away. Instead, it evoked
The wicked, teasing gleam in your

Cold John-Price eyes when I enquired
About your promised project on
My poetry, clinched Hobart as
Too sadistically evil still

For his images to redeem.
Breathtakingly ethereal,
Devoid of folk, this one came close,
Till yet again you crossed my mind.

Sixty Lines For Sixty Years

FAW Tasmania,
A line eight syllables in length,
The same exactly as I use!
I take it as a sign to send

You greetings on your birthday thus,
To celebrate your three score years
With verses such as I have in
My heart to make for you, who'll judge,

As writers do each other, if
My voice is fit to sing your praise.
It comes from far away, from Czech
Republic, where I live these days,

No drawback when your members are
In part like me, refugees from
The fickle spin of fortune's wheel.
Your door wide open to such folk,

Provided that at first they are
Allowed to land and find it so,
At least on entering there to join
They learn that only interest in

The art of writing carries weight.
I owe you much, much more than my
Congratulations can convey,
Since in my troubled youth I knew

Joan Woodberry, former president,
Who published poetry of mine
In fellowship anthologies.
This helped to heal my wounded self-

Esteem incurred when I failed Hell's
Gates' manhood tests, and slabs of steak,
Cooked rare for breakfast, if at all,
On top of last night's skinful caused

My pancreas to twice collapse.
And mercurial Gwen Harwood,
I also had the luck for her
To come my way at the right time.

I called her 'Hardcase', to her face,
Since she, of all the people I
Have glowed with pride to count as friend,
Was least made out of wood, hard, soft,

Smooth-grained, knotty, or otherwise,
Especially her mind-boggling, wit-
Debunking, coruscating head.
When as your leading light she showed

The way through variable seas,
She never pleaded that she was,
With Robyn Mathison's work as
Her secretary, too busy for

A lengthy lunch or fishing trip,
Emergency telephone calls,
Beach walks, epistles and the rest,
Which kept me to my vow to give

Up alcohol for poetry.
But that's another, private tale,
Best left to mystify and tease.
So happy birthday, all the best,

FAW Tasmania.
May you live for as long as there
Are writers needing your support,
Which means forever and a day!

Nightmare in Brown

(There but for the Grace…)

I wake relieved it isn't me,
A man entering a café, all
Eyes on him as he trembles, close

To collapse searching for a free
Big brown old fashioned leather chair,
Squirming to make one cavernous

Enough to snugly fit his booze-
Bloated disintegrating bulk
And give it a measure of peace,

Yield till his shaming plight's not so
Observable to public view.
But well above the arm-rests, his

Left hand grips right wrist to control
The shakes and gulp hairs of the dog,
Cognacs, quickest to steady nerves,

To warm and soothe. And when he calms,
Throat strictures causing spluttering, fear
Of panic overwhelming gone,

He's able comfortably to
Indulge his mood, a study named
After the colour he's sunk in,

Perfect camouflage, and the same
Hue as the sad thin paper bags,
Clingingly damp, the waiter at

The end of. that day's intake clothes
His naked need in to take home.
Rescued from this potential half

A century ago by friends
James McAuley and Gwen Harwood
Who gave me poetry instead,

I'm cured enough to end the dream
Cruelly wondering if he left with
The antique piece wrapped round him still.

Atlas Drive: What's In a Name?

(An interpretation of a nightmare)

Shortly after a suicide
In Atlas Drive, four doors from where
I live, I dreamt I crashed a plane,

In kamikaze style destroyed
All the houses and people there,
And woke wondering if I'd gone mad,

Like Martin Bryant's, my mind too
A deeply warped, embittered hate-
Filled product of Tasmania's in-

Bred rural poor evolved from Van
Diemen's Land's rat-shit origins,
Spared from actually murdering by

The sublimating power of myth:
My often wishing that the giant
Shouldering the burden of the world,

That seems to me a horror show,
Would shrug it off, causing the night
Mare I alone had to endure.

8

After *A Bigger Bonsai 2000*

1

The title alludes to the fact
That this bonsai is on the verge
Of toppling from the yellow moss-

Filled frying pan-shaped tray its dry,
Overcooked sausage-, tortoise neck-
Wrinkled grey trunk's been stuffed into,

My soul shrivelling as I look at
This apology for a tree.
I think too of the skin on arms

We tightened with our hands as kids
To give a 'Chinese burn', of feet
Swaddled to stifle growth, reduce,

Of how I wilted when I first
Saw in Madrid's Retiro Park
Severely limb-lopped Gaudi-like

Coprolite forms confirming of
The label used to try and pin-
Point this folk's national character,

That torture is, as proven by
Their Inquisition, colonies,
And still by matadors with bulls,

'The Spanish Speciality'.
Is it a shrub for mongoloids,
Spastics and others of their kind

To have in their confining cots
As an environment more apt
Than the natural world, its flowers not

Clusters of petals but pink legs
Of insects and the claws of birds
Frustrated on the cramping twists

And turns of crowded branches as
They desperately writhe and seethe
In search of space to freely breathe?

2

It's not politically correct,
But truthfully the image mocks,
Satirises this Japanese

Art form that shrinks, belittles trees,
Distorting them into dwarf shapes
In order to aesthetically

Both compensate and sublimate
For being on average a short,
Even physically stunted race.

And does the witty paradox,
The irony of 'bigger' mean,
Among many other things, that

Their collective, eternal dream
Is to again expand, destroy,
As they did my aunt, a WAAF who

Later in life vanished because
Of them, without trace, as I hope
Will this disturbing, ugly, cruel

Genre too, logically the goal
For its ideal that 'best is small
As possible' to strive to reach.

After *Empty Gesture 1988*

An ocker with a bristling red
Chainsaw head, ugly in his shorts
And singlet showing stunted limbs,

Unnaturally white as though
The sun could never take to them,
With might and main pulls on a rope

Tied round a tree, trying to up-
Root, topple, finish off a growth
Already savagely bonsaied

To resemble his deformed self.
It doesn't yield an inch, but throws
Its shadow as a challenge right

Up to his firmly planted feet,
Like sinisterly lapping sea,
Rising to make him budge instead.

While on an overlooking hill,
Two green saplings, spectators in
This Theatre of the Absurd, shake

Not so much in fear at the thought
Of their possible future as
With helpless laughter at the sight.

After *Gate 1994* (3)

What kind of people would erect,
Withdraw and hope to live behind
This structure that looks more like wires
Strung tautly for a harp some god

Might strum upon than any sort
Of cast-iron barrier, at best
An ornamental fence derived
From fretted, lace-fine, quiver-thin

Black grilles of balconies through which,
As sensitively wrought as them,
The inbred-soon-to-lose-their-heads
Old World aristocrats would peep

At sewer-stricken streets below,
At poverty disease and filth
They never did a thing about?
Transposed to modern times, this split-

Hair, ludicrously flimsy-near-
Invisible foregrounded gate
Is all that keeps out and protects
The folk from mullock mounds as high

And far-flung as a mountain range.
Are they as weirdly rarefied,
Fanatically fashioned as this
Rare hyper-civilised, baroque,

Orchestral instrument, so fey,
Neurotic, decadent, they could
Mistake a gapped expanse of scrolled
Leafage. a pretty see-through screen,

Or wispy, fluttering balustrade
For an effective barricade,
Accept it as their last line of
Defence against encroaching waste?

Do they, obscenely precious, bland,
History-hardened, cynically cool,
Indifferent and urbane, conceive
And then project, as in your work,

The ecologically debased
And troubled Earth as Theatre of
The Absurd, with only a joke
Defence between themselves and it?

After *The Persistence of History 1994*

1

(For John 'Jackie' Dainton)

My great-great grandfather James Sparks
Transported for stealing became
A constable. I see him in

Your painting gunning down a black
Whose only arms are those flung up
As he falls, executed for

Being here first, as hindrance to
The English need to build more gaols
And settle surplus folk abroad.

Imperiously posed with left
Thigh vigorously thrust forth as
He aims and fires, my ancestor's

Shed the broad arrow for Queen's garb
To put him on the side of power
And get a leg up in the world,

The role of punished thief reversed
And he the bully boy instead,
Receiving as a bonus those

Judged even lower than himself
To legally exterminate,
As I betrayed who I was once,

A teased and beaten victim in
Early childhood that went well with
My convict working-class birthright,

Till state school was deserted for
The island's Eton-Harrow, where,
In order to survive, get on,

Instinctively, cap-in-hand, I
Obsequious, sucked up, and when
Promoted to prefect helped mob

A half-caste boy, resulting in,
Since we weren't caned, a lifelong sense
Of discomfort in my own skin.

2

The faded forlorn browns used could
Be early nineteenth century
Sepia hues equating with

The scene's actual date. But the two
Tableau figures, depicted as
Depersonalised, stiff and flat

As silhouettes or fossils stamped
On a Hobart mountain side, would
Be just at home as an image

On an ancient pottery shard, or
A prehistoric cave wall as
Hunter and prey forecasting Cain

And Abel, pure archaisms,
Heraldic emblems, symbols of
High tragedy, such as the Greeks

And Shakespeare wrote, raising them to
A status way beyond a time-
Bound colonial period piece.

3

And theatre plays another role,
Since a fussily elaborate,
Intricately patterned, refined,

Winding and twisting wrought-iron screen
Overlays the frozen image,
Suggestive of an audience

Behind it that would correspond
As emotionally rarefied,
Culturally precious, blasé,

Inbred bloodless sophisticates
Indifferent to what's going on,
People drained of the primitive

As with eye-watering, stifled yawns
Vacantly they await the end
To this all-too-familiar as

To-go-unnoticed murderous act,
For constable and victim to
Thaw out, step forwards, bow, exit,

Release them from a drama where
Poor humans stuck with the same old
Boring natures repeat themselves,

The weak always going down to
The strong, so that they might as well
Go home and put the kettle on.

After *Study For Road In 2002*

An empty unsealed road means no
Impenetrably hard floor of
Darkness between myself and earth,

And bitumen to reinforce
Is out of place when shadows mat,
Stitch lace and coat to bind in strength.

As well they isolate and change
Light into variously shaped
Seemingly cool, transparent pools

I step into in summer on
My long hot walks now that I'm old.
But most invitingly of all

Is the sense that the way ahead
Is unobstructed, and if by
Following this, blind corner turned,

It unfurls further, on and on,
Reprieve from my arrival once
More granted, then I'm filled with joy.

After *End of the Road 2002*

A corner of this life's road turned,
And there it is, I have arrived
At the last stretch of tunnel through
The typically dark woods that could

Entangle still from either side
Before I come out at the stair-
Way leading upwards to a key-
Hole, filled with light of course, as in

The cliché, that's not one when I'm
The person questing for this end
Of being able to unlock
The door and walk into the blaze.

www.ingramcontent.com/pod-product-compliance
Lightning Source LLC
Chambersburg PA
CBHW071021080526
44587CB00015B/2441